Self Promotion Simplified:

Your Guide to Launching a Book

By

Joanne Rock

Dedication

To all of the industry pros who generously contributed to this book, thank you for sharing your time and wisdom with me. Your support means so much.

Table of Contents

Foreword

This guide is not a comprehensive marketing text. It is a focused strategy handbook to help writers launch a book in the (mostly) digital marketplace. *Self Promotion Simplified* is just that—a fast and efficient read that's very specifically targeted to the task, and filled with practical, tested and current advice. This is a user's guide to launching your book successfully and letting the world know it's available. The advice is streamlined for busy writers who need to hit the ground running with their promotional efforts. This guide will help writers to connect with readers, increase their visibility, and start building a long-term readership while maintaining an active writing career.

Introduction

You've written a book! Whether it's your first or your tenth, congratulations to you on the accomplishment. Slogging your way through eighty-thousand words is no small feat and once you reach THE END, you feel very ready to share it with the world. This handbook will help you do just that. A small word of advice though... no matter how ready you think you are to upload your book and start selling copies, there's always time for one more edit.

Remember that each book sells the next

Clean Copy

One of the best self-promotion tactics is to give your readers clean, error-free, engaging copy that they will enjoy. Ask a handful of friends to beta read for you to ensure your work is smooth and the continuity flows. Then, pay a professional editor to give your work another review before you post it. Keep in mind that just because you don't see any more errors doesn't mean they don't exist. As authors, we often introduce errors every time we revise. Worse, because we wrote the book and lived with the characters in our head, we don't always see the story that's on the paper since we can remember other incarnations of the book. Have someone completely new to the story world do your final "closing" edit.

Russ Thompson, Public Relations and Marketing Director of Journalstone Books, reminds authors, "Make sure that the submission is ready for publication. Read it, reread it, and then reread it again. Once you've done that, reread it once more."

Having clean copy with an engaging story is your best promotional tool. If readers like your book, they will look for your work in the future. The opposite is also true. If your work is not polished, you may not get a second chance with the readers. Remember that each book sells the next.

Build Your Backlist

The second piece of easy, upfront advice I can offer you is to write more books. This recommendation was echoed by many industry professionals I interviewed for research. One book is great, but if you write two books, the second book helps sell the first. And book three goes on to help the sales of the prior two. So before you spend money on expensive ads or promotional blog tours, keep in mind that some of the most effective and efficient promotion available is simply *more great books*. If you are at a stage in your career where you can be extremely prolific, run with it. That will drive all your Amazon numbers up when you release each one, especially if you keep your release dates close together.

"New authors, in particular, need to focus on writing first," *New York Times* bestselling author **Dianna Love** explains. "Until you have a backlist of at least three or more books, don't put a lot of time or money into promoting. Use your available marketing time to build name awareness – social networking, live events, street team development – so that when you do launch a major campaign to promote your books, some of the audience will recognize your name. One mistake I often see is a writer with her first book putting a tremendous focus on promoting that one book. Whether it's indie or traditionally published, the best way to promote yourself is by writing more books."

If, however, you are ready to use a different part of your brain while your Muse recovers from the last manuscript, I invite you to spend some time promoting the book you've just written in my "Pick Your Launch Plan" approach to promotion.

A Word about Choosing a Launch Plan

This book is divided into "Launch Plans" based on how much lead time you have before your book is released. If you are writing a three-book series, it might be wise to give yourself plenty of time before you release Book 1 so that you can release all three books close together—perhaps a month or two apart. That's a good reason to choose the long-range launch plan so you have more time to write, plus you'll have more time to put together a comprehensive launch for your book or series.

Even if you are ready to release your book next week and you need to move right into the faster, short range plan, still read through the ideas in the long-term strategy section as I've included some foundational building blocks for promotion in this section. Familiarize yourself with the ideas so you can start incorporating those strategies before your next work is released.

Effective promotion and social media relations are built over time. It's crucial to think about your brand and how you want to market that brand to readers so that all your future projects and promotional efforts can reflect that concept. Or ask a friend to help you accomplish some of the additional launch strategies to increase your reach.

Don't miss the Resources section at the end of this book. The list compiles websites and vendors mentioned in the text, and the digital version of *Self Promotion Simplified* contains hyperlinks to many of them.

The One Year Launch Plan

Ideally, you have the luxury of really planning the promotional strategy of your first book or series of books. As exciting as it may be to see your first story available for sale, it might be a good idea to build in a little time before you release it (if you're self-publishing) to plot your promotional strategy. If you've sold your book to a traditional press, chances are you have several months before the work is available. Literary Agent **Barbara Collins Rosenberg** of The Rosenberg Group cautions new authors, "The work doesn't stop, in fact, it's just beginning because you should be writing a second book, while getting your name out to your potential audience. Before speaking with your editor and publicist about what the house will do to promote your title, study what other authors are doing with their websites, their blogs, their contests, their twitter feeds, to get an idea of what you're comfortable with and what works for your target audience. Then, when you engage with your assigned publicist, make sure that he or she knows that you are there to aid and augment their efforts."

This advice brings out an important, often overlooked component in new authors' promotional strategies—research. It pays to watch the way successful authors network online and build their fan bases. What strategies work for them? Is there anything you can emulate or incorporate into your own effort? In addition to doing some research, here are other things to be thinking about in the year before your release:

- Brand message
- Promotional toolkit
- Comprehensive web-presence
- Street team or other promotional network
- Live events

Brand message

An author brand is determined by the product you deliver to your readers. If you are already a multi-published author it is easier for you to look back at a body of work and identify the kinds of books you've brought to market in the past.

Deb Werksman, Editorial Manager of Sourcebooks, reinforces the importance of branding for her authors. "The most important thing an author can do is to position the book properly so that every piece of the packaging—title, subtitle, cover design—and marketing speaks directly to the reader and communicates 'must read'. To do this well, the author has to do a lot of market research, and most difficult, get out of her own story and think from the point of view of the reader. Readers have many choices about where to spend their time and money. What makes your book stand out?"

To accomplish this, ask yourself what makes your books unique from other authors' work in the same sub-genre? Identify the qualities that make your work different. A romance author might brand her work—"Fresh, flirty, fun!" Or a suspense author might promise readers "Stories to keep you awake at night."

In the above examples, I've turned the brand message into a tag line. You don't have to do this—it can be enough for you to understand your brand and get across the idea through your packaging. But if you know your brand and the inherent promise you make to your readers, it will help you to craft cover art, website banners and a social media presence that all support the brand. If your promise is "fresh, flirty and fun" don't confuse the message by posting a haunted house on your Facebook cover page just for fun. Your Halloween theme might lean more toward a cartoon of someone wearing a flirty kitten costume. If you write heart-pounding suspense, think targets, badges, and guns. Be consistent and reinforce the brand. Readers absorb the message over time.

For a fantastic example of branding, take a look at *USA Today* bestselling author **Catherine Mann's** website at catherinemann.com. Her concept of "Rescued by Love" helps readers see her romantic books support animal rescue, a message underscored by paw prints and hearts. In this case, it's not just the words that convey the idea, it's the images. Even her author photo—complete with her dog–sends a message about her books.

Spend some time researching authors' brands who write in a subgenre similar to yours for ideas that work (or don't!) and you will start to gather ideas for defining your brand. Write your brand message on a sticky note to post above your computer. All your promotional efforts need to underscore this message.

Tips for finding your brand:

If you've published before, read your favorite reviewers' comments on your books. Highlight your favorite lines or key phrases that describe your writing. Your reviewers might have already described what makes your work unique.

Show a personal side to your readers

If you are publishing for the first time, write a list of the qualities you hope are in your work. Then, ask some beta readers to describe or review your work and see how their perspective is the same or different than yours. What kinds of phrases do people use most often to describe your work?

Melissa Jeglinski, Literary Agent for The Knight Agency, offers some additional insights on building a brand as an author, "No matter what you do, always show a personal side to your readers. That doesn't mean all of your life's details need to be shared. But give them little insights into who you are as you promote your book. Are you passionate about certain charities or issues? Do you craft? Are your pets hilariously photogenic? Focus on one thing so they'll remember you're the author who does all that work for children's charities or the one who makes personalized jewelry. And when you promote your book you can work that unique thing about you into it so it's not just all about selling in their minds."

Promotional toolkit

Once you know your brand, you're ready to start developing some of the key components of your writer's promotional toolkit. Some of the standard components of any writer's promotions are an author bio, basic press release and a good author photo.

Photo

First, invest in some good color as well as black and white photos of yourself. A professional photo does not come cheap, but it is worth the investment. This is not to say the pricier the better. Compare a few professional studios to familiarize yourself with the rates and see what you can negotiate. If you have a friend who is skilled with a camera, that might be fine, but see what kind of results you get before you commit to using their photos.

Do not be tempted to skimp on this crucial promotional tool. Newspapers will shy away from reprinting your color photo from last weekend's camping trip in their paper if it's too much work to make if fit their specifications. And you definitely want your photo to run with an article about you wherever and whenever possible because it will draw more readers to the story. Even if they do not read the piece, they will look at the photo and your name.

The photo will be used and re-used on your website, in all your social media profiles, on your publisher's website if you have one, and on your Amazon and Goodreads profile. Plus you'll want pictures to send around with your press releases about your latest news. I recommend a range of photos so you have more than one stock picture to choose from. Get some outdoor shots or photos in your work space so that readers feel like they are connecting with you personally. But it's a good idea to have some photos with a neutral background as well, which might be necessary for a speaker's bio or conference program.

Finally, be sure the size of your photo meets quality requirements for both print and web reproduction. You'll want sharp, clear pics for print with over 1000 pixels x over 1000 pixels, whereas for web use, you can offer photos at about 200px x 300px. However, **Cissy Hartley**, Owner and Founder of Writerspace, reminds authors that "Pixel size isn't the only consideration for print. Resolution is just as important or more so. Web photos are fine at 72 dpi (dots per inch). However, if you had a 1000 x 1000 pixel image that was 72 dpi, it still wouldn't work for print. An image needs to be at least 300 dpi for print quality."

Author Bio

After you've secured good photos for use online and in print, you'll want a good author bio. Now is not the time to be modest. In third person narrative include your publishing credits (although if these are numerous, consider attaching a complete list of books on a separate sheet), awards, organizations and memberships, education, hometown, current city or region of residence, how long you've been writing, and writing related activities, such as teaching or giving seminars. *See Figure 1 for a quick how-to.*

A good bio needs to be updated yearly and occasionally tweaked for your audience. A speaker's bio reads more professionally than what you'd use at the back of your current fiction release. A bio for readers should be friendly and engaging, whereas a press kit bio focuses more on your achievements. It can be helpful also to keep a short and long bio in your files to meet the needs of editors, journalists or conference organizers who request a certain length.

Press Release

Newspapers, television and radio are tried and true media outlets and they will be important targets for your writing news. Equally important for you are e-zines, internet radio stations and book blogs, and all of those outlets are great targets for press releases too.

A press release can work for you in a lot of ways. You can email it to newspapers (targeted to the features editor or book reviews contact), send it out to radio stations while lobbying for an on-air interview, or you can post the press release on your website as part of your electronic media kit so that interested parties can download at will. It is worth updating a press release often so the information stays current.

Write a new press release each time you have a book out or an event to promote. Since a press release is sent to media outlets it must have news value. **Regina Luttrell**, an Assistant Professor at Eastern Michigan University who specializes in public relations and social media, points out that, "'Newsworthiness' defines the impact the story has on a specific audience and how that audience will be influenced. Do your research to identify which journalist will be receptive to your press release. A common mistake with a novice who attempts to work with journalists is sending out the same release to several journalists at the same media outlet. This is called 'shotgunning,' and this tactic turns journalists off. Don't risk ruining your relationship before it's even begun."

Be sure your release is relevant to whatever media outlet you are targeting. Don't send out a blanket press release to every outlet on your target list. Start with a basic release and then tailor it for each individual outlet. Think of this document as a sample article that could run in a newspaper about you or your book. Give your press release a title that reads like a newspaper headline. Examples: "Local Author to Speak at Fiction Workshop," or "New Book Set in Omaha" (if you are sending to the Omaha paper). Write a story in the traditional journalism-style inverted pyramid to fit the headline. Also keep in mind that newspaper editors almost always cut copy from the bottom, so hit the highlights in the first few sentences. Sometimes papers or magazines with small staffs will run your story verbatim if your press release is well targeted. *See Figure 2 for how-to.*

Once you've written your press release, you want it to do as much work as possible for you.

Use the Promotion Target List (*Figure 3*) to help brainstorm a list of places to contact regarding your news. Don't send out a release addressed to the newsroom or to "editor." Be sure you have a contact name even if it means calling the newspaper and doing some quick research. Keep your contacts list up to date from year to year.

After sending your press releases, follow up with your contacts to be sure they've received the information. Don't be a nuisance—repeated calls and emails are unwelcome and unnecessary. You can't coerce a story and you want to maintain good relations. However, editors are busy and might appreciate a quick reminder before your event.

Other Promo Tools

Today's journalist uses social media regularly to connect with sources

Besides the photo, bio and press release, there are a few other items you can add to an online (or print) media kit if you choose. Add a picture of your cover along with the book blurb, ISBN #, and review quotes from other authors if you have them. You can also include a Top Ten list for interest. For example, if you've set a book in a real seaside resort town, you can add a list of local bed and breakfasts or a list of top ten ways to spend the day according to local tourists. The list can be fun and should reflect the tone of your book. Likewise, if you've written a suspense set in a fictional abandoned hotel, you could include a list of top properties reputed to be haunted in the United States. Pieces like this add interest to your press kit and might entice a reader to stop and spend more time on your material. If your press kit is digital, hyperlinks to the places you've listed are a welcome bonus. Assistant Professor **Regina Luttrell** reminds us, "Be sure to include your Twitter ID or other social sites you maintain. Today's journalist uses social media regularly to connect with sources."

A few more ideas for the press kit / promotional toolkit include: fact sheets about your genre, your setting or your books, a complete book list with ISBN numbers, bookmark, a list of links to your social media and websites, and a business card.

Comprehensive web presence

Another important facet of your promotional plan is developing a digital presence for fans to find and connect with you. Think about your website as your home's living room—the place where you entertain your guests. It should be welcoming and easy to navigate. Guests should feel at home and want to stay awhile, so make sure you have plenty to engage them and keep them occupied. In your real house, you'd hang some personal pictures, some interesting artwork, and maybe put out a board game or a great coffee table book. Your website should also include personal pics, engaging art, and maybe some trivia or a game. Give visitors a reason to linger.

You can pay for website development and get help with this. But building your own site is cheaper if you have a vision of what you want. I use ipage for my YA books, but many authors I know set up websites through word press or blog spot and create a site around their blog. Social media expert **Regina Luttrell** suggests, "Wix.com is another free resource available to authors. With sleek designs and an easy-to-use, easy-to-understand content management system, creating your own site is quick and simple."

Before setting up a website, surf the net for other author websites you enjoy. Make notes about what works and doesn't work. Some sites overdo the music, graphics and badges so that it becomes difficult to focus on the primary content. Some sites use color combinations of font/background that hurt your eyes or make it difficult to read for long periods of time. I am of the mindset that clean and simple is better than too busy, but balance this need for clarity with style elements that reflect your writing voice.

Beyond the style of your site, you should make notes on what buttons are essential. You'll want to link to all your books, of course. But do you wish to sell on your site? Do you want to direct readers to Goodreads, Amazon and/or Barnes and Noble? Again, see what other authors do before you start posting links galore.

In addition to purchase links or links to your book details, you'll want an author bio available on your site. This one can be more friendly and engaging—more personal—than the one you sent out in your press kit. Connect with readers by sharing something about yourself whether that's a favorite pastime or a glimpse of your home office or a funny Q & A with you or one of your pets. Readers come to your site to learn more about you, so infuse your site with your personality.

Other must-haves on a website include buttons to contact you in multiple ways—via email, via various social media, or through a contact form on the site—as well as a newsletter sign up if you're going to have one. If you blog, link to your blog and maybe a roll call of your favorite blogs that you frequent.

Be sure to include social media links prominently as some readers prefer to connect via Twitter or Instagram. I'd have the social media links on every page of the site so that no matter where your reader lands, they see them prominently.

To Blog or Video-log

I find daily blogging takes away too much time from fiction writing, so I don't do this. I like to join group blogs so that I have a consistent blog date somewhere once a month and then save my other blogging efforts for blog tours when I have a book releasing. If, however, you enjoy blogging or vlogging, it's a great way to connect with readers. Study the authors who do this well and consistently to get ideas for yours. Be sure your blog reflects your brand and the look of your website if they are not hosted in the same spot.

Editorial Director of ImaJinn Books, **Brenda Chin**, has some great insights for beginning bloggers or anyone looking for a stronger sense of direction with their author blog. "Ask yourself what you bring to the table that nobody else can? A great example of an author using her uniqueness to entertain her readers and sell a lot of books is *New York Times* bestselling author **Jill Shalvis**. If you've ever read any of

Jill's books, you know that the characters are just like you and me. They feel like friends. Jill, herself, comes across as someone you'd love to hang out with. One of her most successful tools is a blog. There she posts pictures of her family, her pets, as well as the frequent bears who come to check out her garbage. While she sometimes talks about her books, she's just as likely to tell you her latest I Love Lucy adventure, or an embarrassing thing she did while attempting to snag a few cookies. She comes across as very real and a lot of fun. And readers buy her books for the same kind of entertainment they sample in her blog."

If you prefer not to blog, or if you'd like to try it but aren't sure you can make the time commitment to creating as much content as a blog requires, you can try micro-blogging on a site like Tumblr. I'm a big fan of Tumblr for the visual aspect. For me, this network combines the appeal of Pinterest and blogging as it gives me the chance to connect with readers briefly and more frequently than my blog appearances.

Another option for less frequent blogging is to host your author blog on Goodreads, which has a built in tool for this. Time spent on Goodreads seems to be rewarded by its visitors, so check this out. I find it less user friendly than other tools as it takes longer to size pictures properly or add eye-catching content, but they may update this in the near future. For now I'm linking my Tumblr blog into the Goodreads blog tool. This lets you link an RSS feed, which in turn allows the information from one site to feed into another. This is very easy to do. Just search for "how to find the RSS feed" for whatever blog you want to show up on your Goodreads page, and follow the easy instructions.

*When readers Google
your name, often the first
link to you and your
work is your Amazon
author page, so make
your profile there as
complete and engaging
as possible*

Goodreads/Amazon Author pages

You need approval from both Goodreads and Amazon in order to create author pages on their sites. When you see your book go up, look for the spot on the page that says something like "Are you the author of this book?" Request these pages as soon as your links to your book go live on their sites as you'll want to create a presence as engaging as your own website in these forums. When readers Google your name, often the first link to you and your work is your Amazon author page, so make your profile there as complete and engaging as possible. This may be as far as readers go in their search for information. Post pictures, add your Twitter feed to your Amazon page, add the RSS feed to your blog, post a video, a bio, and any upcoming book signings or appearances. Update your Amazon author page often.

Goodreads has similar features on their author pages as Amazon, but on Goodreads you also have the option to interact with the community. Another bonus of Goodreads is that you can start a "reader" profile page even before your book link is available and then transfer that reader profile to your author page once you are approved as an author. This allows you to start building your connections sooner. Your books must be listed on Goodreads in order for you to request to be a Goodreads Author. If you don't see it listed, you can add it yourself and then submit your request. The "Goodreads Author" program opens up some more opportunities for connecting with your fans.

On Goodreads, your friends will see what books are on your shelf and whose work you enjoy reading. I urge you to explore this huge community. You can post trivia quizzes about your book and giveaways of your recent releases. Goodreads is a good venue to help you build a base of reader reviews. If you post a giveaway, for example, the readers who win your books are prompted to post reviews afterward. In addition, there are communities of readers who discuss every variety of literary subgenre in the forums. Join some groups, post a little bit about topics besides your book (although a self-serving post about your book is certainly fine in the right venue!) and you'll gain some friends, fans and reviews.

Social Media Sites

As time allows before your book releases, set up dedicated author pages on the social media sites you enjoy. If you haven't explored social media communities yet, do this as soon as possible. If you're unsure, you can do an Internet search for the top ten social media sites, which at the time of writing included Facebook, Twitter, Pinterest, LinkedIn, Google + and Tumblr, all sites that I'm currently using and enjoy. I'm not on Instagram as I don't have an iPhone, but I'd be there if I did as the community is active and I like all the pictures. I hope to check out Meet Up soon too, which a writer friend mentioned to me recently as the way she connected with her local writers' group.

There are a lot of social media options. Take your time thinking through which places best suit your needs. **Brenda Chin** of ImaJinn Books points out, "It can be confusing and with the way the market's changing, nobody knows what will work for long. I don't claim to know any marketing secrets, but I do advise my authors to have their own web page, and to take advantage of as many social media possibilities as they can. If you can do Facebook, Twitter, Pinterest, etc., do them. But tomorrow there might be a better way." In other words, keep an eye on social media trends, but there's no need to follow them slavishly. Try new spots that sound interesting to you for socializing online. Stick with the ones you enjoy most and be ready to branch out as readers move elsewhere.

Only commit to as much social media as you feel comfortable with. If you have limited time for social media or don't trust yourself to follow through on multiple sites, try and be active on two and see how you do there before you build more. Once I started participating on Twitter, it intersected with so many other sites that I found myself stopping by other authors' pages on various social media more often and I began to see what ones appealed to me.

As with your Amazon and Goodreads pages, take the time to build a nice home base for yourself on each social media site you frequent. Craft an attractive cover page photo for your Facebook Author Page as well as your Twitter home page. Make sure your bio and links are up to date. Include a profile photo of your face. While some authors are reluctant to do this, I know that readers like to see YOU somewhere on your pages when they look up your work, so I encourage a good photo of yourself as an icon.

Being relevant and in sync with your market creates meaningful engagement opportunities

Social Media Engagement / Content

Once you've established your presence, the real work of day to day interaction begins. **Robert Manasier**, CEO of In Focus Brands, has some advice for tackling this effectively as an author, "You need to be clear as to your book's true target market; who are you talking to and who will listen. Being relevant and in sync with your market creates meaningful engagement opportunities. At this stage, "selling" the benefits of reading/downloading your specific book is your audience catch."

Next, participate as much as you feel comfortable while still maintaining your writing schedule. Social media can be fun but it can also quickly steal away your work time, so set a timer if you need to. (Or if you don't love social media, maybe you'll need the timer to be sure you're putting in enough time!) But comment on some other posts related to your genre, share things that interest you, that relate to your books, or that relate to your characters. If you're writing action heroes with military connections, post news snippets related to real service members engaged in the same types of jobs.

As always, Follow/Friend/Fan the writers who are in your genre and whose work you enjoy. You'll learn from the kinds of things they post and the way they interact with their readers. Don't hesitate to become involved in their reader communities as you *are* their reader. While you don't want to hawk your own books on their pages, participation and a presence is always appreciated by other authors. If others in the community like what you have to say, they'll most certainly click on your icon and find out more about you.

Multi-media

I like to be on several social media sites because I genuinely enjoy the chance to connect with readers. I also enjoy using more than one social network since I like to appeal to readers through text, pictures and video since some readers prefer one over the other.

You may find it nerve-wracking to introduce yourself to readers in a video, but keep in mind that fans are anxious to find out more about writers whose book they enjoy. Post a video on YouTube, link to it on Amazon and Goodreads and on your website so that readers can feel like they are meeting you. If you'd rather not have a casual chat with the camera, ask a friend to interview you about your work, or you can read a favorite scene from your manuscript. The point is to let readers see you speaking and engaging with them.

At the same time, weigh the benefits of "casual" versus sloppy. **Alfred Antico**, Ph.D., Associate Professor of Communications at The College of Saint Rose in Albany NY cautions that "While you can use audio and video podcasts on your website and in other social media to sustain your connection, they aren't necessarily do-it-yourself projects. Things such as poor lighting and sound can quickly undermine your credibility. Hire a professional who can work with you to direct your performances and create a distinct sound and look for you; someone who you trust to provide honest critique."

Some writers have done really creative things with their author videos from giving tours of their gardens to tours of the downtown where their book is set, or acting out a funny scene with their kids or their friends. Whatever you decide to do, it's just another way for readers to meet you and feel like a part of your story world.

After you post a "Meet the Author" video, consider a book video. If you've got a budget for this, you can hire a company to create a book trailer for you or you can create one on your own if you have a movie maker on your computer and some creativity to bring to the table (See the Three-Month Launch Plan for more on this). You may find this a fun and creative outlet to bring your story to life. Be sure to obtain permission for any images or music you use or purchase stock art online.

As with any new piece you create, be sure to tout it on your social media outlets and post it on your website and blog. Every new tool you develop to promote you and your work should start feeding into the outlets you've developed before so that you're growing your presence and using your existing community to build a bigger following.

Street Teams

You may be tempted to start a street team or other promotional group to help you spread the word about your books. An enthusiastic group who wants to share your writing news online or in person may sound like a great idea—and it can be!—but overseeing this kind of community takes time and is a long term commitment so think carefully about how much time you have to devote to your team before starting.

I recommend talking to other authors who have a street team or even joining another author's street team so you can see how one is run from the inside. How are they keeping their teams engaged between releases? How much participation is expected from group members to stay in the group? Is a new group recruited for each release or can members remain in the group for years?

These are all questions you'll want to think through, in addition to what kinds of promo items or swag you will give to team members. For example, how will you award swag items? Some authors give a welcome package to all team members while others award promo items for contest prizes. Either way can work, but you'll want to think about how much you can afford for giveaways and team swag before you announce highly coveted gear to every member. Also, you will have team members requesting to help you in foreign countries which can be a wonderful way to build some awareness in overseas markets, but the postage for shipping abroad is very expensive. One way to avoid this is to send books through sites like Book Depository or Better World Books, which offer free shipping to many overseas countries.

If you have time and can personally oversee a street team at least for the first few months, a group like this can be invaluable for multiplying your social network outreach and spreading the word to readers about your work. Dedicated readers are worth their weight in gold, both for their enthusiasm for the books and for their access to other readers who share their tastes. You'll quickly see that these connections are worth the swag and more! Find fun ways to reward your team for their efforts by polling them about what kinds of swag they'd like to have or what kinds of events they would enjoy promoting.

Give the group some buy-in and they will be all the more invested in your projects.

Promo Items

As you consider promotional items for your street team, contest giveaways and mailings to readers, think about the cost of creating the item, the shelf life of the item and the cost of shipping the item. For example, a bookmark for your first book has less longevity than a bookmark for a series. You might wait to create a bookmark until you have firm release dates and possibly cover art for more than one book.

Weigh the benefits of inexpensive promo items. While it's great to have a large quantity of giveaway material, is it worth the cost if the item has very little value to readers? Order some less expensive giveaways for book signings and order a smaller number of higher quality swag items as contest giveaways or incentive prizes available for your street team or the readers online who share your news and tout your books.

There are many options for ordering promotional giveaways. I've listed some in the Resources section of this guide that I've used personally, but you may find the best prices at a local vendor. Price compare and don't hesitate to request samples before you buy. You save money per piece when you buy in bulk, but be careful of ordering a thousand items with a short shelf life. Also be careful of investing too much of your budget in bookmarks and print materials as they are less coveted by readers.

Finally, you can offer website visitors the option of ordering their own promo items directly from a storefront if you use Cafe Press, a company that allows you to design and sell your own merchandise. The items are pricier than if you order in bulk, of course, but it allows enthusiastic fans to order more swag and maybe even design some of their own. Also, if you get into a bind and run out of t-shirts, it's nice to be able to order just a couple of them quickly through a service like this, or to order them from Cafe Press and have the store ship them directly to contest winners for you.

Live Events

A longer lead time is essential for setting up quality live events. If you would like to do a launch party for your book, booksellers need months in advance to organize this, advertise it to their readers and order books. Approach booksellers at least three months in advance, but you might need longer than that to really plan the launch month if you want to do multiple live events.

Check with your bookseller before you sign remaining stock, but this is usually an effective way to sell leftover copies afterward

If you don't mind traveling, a small book tour might be a good idea if you think you can generate some traffic. If you've never done a book signing before, be warned they can be lonely events unless you've got some friends who plan to attend! Don't let a quiet book signing disappoint you too much, though. Book sellers have told me that they usually sell more of the author's book *after* the signing for a variety of reasons. Customers sometimes can't make it to the store that day or they forgot about it and will buy the book the next time they are in the store. Other times, customers will circle your table but don't like to feel "on the spot" to buy something if they approach you. Those same readers, however, are likely to look for your book another time they are in the store or tell their friends they saw a signing. Check with your bookseller before you sign remaining stock, but this is usually an effective way to sell leftover copies afterward. Bring some "Autographed by the author" stickers with you and ask the bookseller about placement of the stickers. Sometimes the stores prefer to use their own stickers, or sometimes they can tell you if they prefer your stickers on the spine versus the cover. Always follow their preference as they sell the books!

In addition, you can often sign stock in your local bookstores even if you aren't doing a formal book signing. Stop by area booksellers when your release debuts and let them know you'd like to sign their stock or leave behind some bookmarks. This is usually warmly welcomed, but it is always best to introduce yourself and ask first.

Promote It

If you decide to do a signing, don't rely solely on the bookseller to promote your event. You need to promote it on Goodreads, Amazon and in all your social media venues. If you have a publisher, ask them to promote the event as well. In addition, prepare to create a real experience for your readers when they attend the signing. In other words, you should do more than show up with a pen unless you are a huge bestseller with an active publicist.

Giveaways

Authors try to create engaging tables with take-away material for browsing readers. This can include bookmarks or other promo items like buttons, pins, pens, or something related to your book. For our Young Adult books in the Camp Boyfriend series, my co-author **Karen Rock** and I give away friendship bracelets and temporary tattoos that say "I [heart] Camp." A quick trip to websites that specialize in promo items will give you some ideas for giveaways. If you're on a budget, don't overlook the power of candy. You can pick up a bag of lollipops or candy at the drugstore and generate as much traffic to your table with the promise of sugar, although you don't get the bonus of having your reader take something home with your name on it.

Visual interest

You can purchase a colorful table drape to coordinate with your cover and jazz up the space. Create visual interest with materials of varying heights. Add a display case that holds a few books upright or bring a giveaway basket full of fun things related to your book. You can ask readers to sign up for your newsletter and they will be entered to win the basket. Or just give tickets away for the basket as a door prize at the end of the signing and remind people they have to be present to win.

Authors who have a series out and will be promoting multiple events in the series might invest in a banner for their table front. These come in standard sizes, are easy to hang and help readers see your book covers and message even if they are too shy to come over to your table. This might be especially helpful for an erotica author who might have some readers who don't advertise their love of racy books. Having a sign with your name on it will help you broadcast your message so your reader can go home and download your book privately.

Promote Some More

Finally, be sure to use your press kit and a press release to spread the word about all book signings and author appearances. One of the biggest rewards of live events is not book sales as much as the possibility of press coverage and exposure. Have a friend take photos of the event and send them to the paper afterward if your local paper did not cover the event. It doesn't hurt to send a follow-up press release after the event. Also, those photos are valuable for use on your website and in social media. Just be sure to take a few different kinds of photos to appeal to various audiences—some with readers and fans, images of you with your books, pictures of you speaking in front of a group or interacting more directly with attendees. Small town weekly newspapers/shoppers are always looking for ways to boost local content and your event coverage may be just the right content and size to fill their news space. Emailing a JPG with the article and photo both in the body of the email and as attachments will make their jobs even easier, increasing the likelihood of your press release being published.

The Three-Month Launch Plan

A three-month window allows you to develop some key tools for a book launch. Some of these tasks can be hired out to specialized companies to save you time and energy, but be careful of overspending on a book's launch. Some authors set aside a portion of their advance for promotions, but if you're self-publishing a first book, you might want to be very conservative with a budget until the book starts to sell. If you've self-published multiple books and have an idea what to expect for income, you might limit yourself to 15% of expected earnings for promotion. This conservative approach favors writing in a series since you can earn some income from book one and use a percentage of those earnings to promote book two, which in turn should boost your book one sales as well.

Here are some ideas for spreading the word about your book three months prior to release:

- Blog tour
- Pre-order incentives
- Cover Reveal
- Newsletter
- Book video
- Advance reviews
- Web presence: Three months prior to launch

Blog Tour

A blog tour is a series of appearances on book blogger websites to discuss your book, offer behind-the-scenes glimpses of the creative process, offer character interviews and other special insights on your story. A blog tour might be a place to save yourself a little time and energy since it's a simple portion to hand off to a professional tour company. There are many groups who can execute this well for a reasonable fee. You can find prospective tour companies by visiting your favorite blogs and seeing if they are "tour hosts" for any of the blog companies. This is frequently advertised in the form of digital badges running down a column of the blog. Ask other author friends about companies they like.

A professional blog tour company can solicit blogs for you to make appearances for a one or two week tour (or longer if you prefer), they gather the information and necessary hyperlinks to send the bloggers and make sure the content goes live in a timely fashion. They promote the tour, often create a banner graphic for the event, and can help you with a tour-wide giveaway.

If you are putting your release on the line, then respect what people will say

Lisa Filipe, creator of Tasty Blog Tours, is experienced at guiding new authors through an online tour, but she cautions new authors to manage their expectations for what a blog tour can offer them in terms of promotion. "Book tours are only a promotional tool to help get your release in front of new readers or pre-existing fans. They are not a way to get 'five star' reviews on Amazon/B&N/Goodreads. If you are putting your release on the line, then respect what people will say. You can't grow as a writer if no one ever tells you the truth."

Filipe also suggests that authors come to their blog tour host with all the necessary support materials in place, especially the cover art and blurb. "The Cover will attract the eye of the reader like a shiny penny. You need it to stand out, but also represent what is inside the pages. And a good blurb, short and to the point is always best. If the blurb drags on and on, it's called a synopsis. Make it sharp, quick and stick to the story as best as possible, using key points."

However, be careful of overcommitting yourself to something like this as it can require far more time and energy than you may realize at first glance. Often, blog tours require a fair amount of original content—generated by you—to offer to the various blogs. You can write some pieces in advance. But some blogs have a list of questions for you that need to be addressed individually and often need to be completed in a short amount of time. Writing material for the blogs can take hours away from the rest of your writing. Be certain that you want to use your writing time this way.

In addition to the time spent creating content, a good blog tour thrives with author participation. Will you enjoy visiting each blog and finding ways to tout the content in your social media outlets? Will you take the time to thank each blogger, comment on their posts and spend some meaningful time on their blogs? For some authors, this is a fun way to creatively recharge and it makes sense to engage with blogs and their followers. But if you don't have the time to follow through on this end of the tour, you might ask yourself if you're getting as much out of the experience as possible. If the answer is no, start with something simpler—like a blitz event or release event—and work your way up to a larger blog tour. (More on blitz events in the One Month Plan.) You can also ask a tour company about arranging a "Review Tour" for the book where the bloggers receive copies of the book to review and the participants focus on reviewing the book as opposed to using content generated by the author.

Promote the bloggers in your social media during the tour, thank them afterward, and … maintain a good relationship

Whatever you decide to do, be sure to promote the bloggers in your social media during the tour, thank them afterward, and if you like their blogs, be sure to follow/friend them to maintain a good relationship. For social media shout-outs, I like to take screen shots of the blogs and post pictures on my Tumblr or Pinterest, always posting a link back to the blog. You can also add a line of teaser copy or pull out a question that is answered in the interview and try to generate some traffic that way.

Pre-order Incentives

There are pros and cons to promoting pre-orders for your book. In the traditional publishing model, pre-orders were great as they could help sway bookstores to order more copies or persuade your publisher to increase a print run, or any number of good things. Encouraging your readers to pre-order was a given.

However, in an era of tremendous self-publishing growth, authors might choose not to encourage pre-orders since Amazon does not count pre-order sales toward their bestseller stats. In other words, authors are of course credited with the sale and earn the income, but they don't receive the boost of realizing all the pre-order sales in whatever mathematics dictate the Amazon bestseller lists. At least, not as of this writing. I'd watch online for discussions of this issue as it seems like this could change in the not too distant future.

If you choose to encourage your readers to pre-order your book, consider offering some kind of value-added incentive. Can they receive a bonus gift directly from you for pre-ordering? Higher profile authors find that independent booksellers can be accommodating about special promotions like this, advertising it in their store newsletters and generating buzz since it's something the chain stores or Amazon can't coordinate. But even smaller authors might find a local bookstore that would be happy to arrange a pre-order promotion. Perhaps if your readers buy a book through X store, they will receive a download code for a free novella. Sometimes authors offer stickers or a bookmark along with their autograph on all pre-ordered copies. Think about something fun and different to offer them. You might only sell twenty copies this way, but you might sell many more. The bigger benefit might be from bookseller good will and a reason to talk about your book in social media outlets in the weeks leading up to the release.

Take a photo of whatever you will be offering your readers as an incentive gift and post it in on your website and blog along with your social media outlets. The visual of the prize is always a bonus. Be explicit in your instructions regarding how a reader needs to pre-order the book in order to obtain the gift. Also, it's imperative to follow through in a timely fashion to make sure the orders are met and that readers receive their gifts/books quickly. If that means setting aside a day before the book comes out to visit the bookseller who is sponsoring the pre-order initiative, plan for this in your schedule.

When weighing the cost of the pre-order promotion, be sure to take into account the expense of postage for the gifts in addition to the bonus gifts themselves. You might be surprised at how this adds up, especially if you've allowed international readers to pre-order as well. If you think your book might attract a strong overseas readership, look into postage for those long distance mailings ahead of time or consider making the pre-order incentive a bonus for domestic readers.

Finally, consider adding a personal note to all your mail-outs, whether it's a sticky note or a personalization in signing the book. That personal contact with your readers goes farther to create a good relationship than any other gift you send.

Cover Reveal

The timing for a book cover "reveal" varies widely. A traditional publishing house may want to unveil your cover as early as six or seven months before the release date so that the book is in the sales catalog for advance sales. That's a good thing, of course, but if your cover is already up on online, you've lost your window for a big reveal. Plan farther ahead for your next book and coordinate with your publisher to that you can take advantage of this easy bit of extra promotion for you book.

If you're self-publishing the piece, or if your small press allows you some flexibility, you can publicize your cover much closer to the release date and use the cover reveal event as a way to generate buzz about the release. Schedule a date anywhere from three months to two weeks prior to your on-sale date. You can go onto your social media sites to ask bloggers if they would be interested in participating in your cover reveal, or hire a blog tour company to coordinate the effort for you. The charge for a cover event is considerably smaller than a blog tour, so this might be an easy way for you to save time, take advantage of the tour company's blogger network, and gain some more visibility.

Either way, you'll need to have a high resolution, high quality cover image ready to share. Package up additional information to send out with the cover including the ISBN and buy links, sale date and book genre, book blurb, your social media links, an author photo and bio. Send all of this to your participating bloggers several days before the reveal date. The extra time—as opposed to waiting until the night before the event—is a thoughtful courtesy since many busy bloggers prefer to upload material to their blog in batches one or two days a week instead of on a daily basis. As always, thank your participants profusely as their help here is vital. Also, the easier and more fun you make the event for them this time, the more likely they will be to participate in your future author events.

Newsletter

An author newsletter is a valuable tool. The sooner you can begin to build a mailing list, the better. Offer incentives to your readers for signing up by creating "subscriber only" contests or exclusive sneak peeks at a work in progress, whatever might entice people to opt in for your reader list. Connect with your newsletter subscribers in the same way you engage fans on social media. Be personal, be true to your brand and give them something special they won't find in your books.

Some authors offer readers book recommendations with excerpts or blurbs about other authors' stories their readers might like. Other ideas include sharing deleted scenes, character interviews, or photos from research trips. An author newsletter doesn't even have to focus solely on books, especially if you combine your passion for a hobby in your books. In other words, if you write military books, you might feature unique military jobs, or interesting defense technology, anything you've been studying for your writing. Sign up for some other authors' mailing lists to see what other writers are doing and get a feel for what kinds of content you enjoy.

Mailing List Tools

Research mailing list software providers to see which will best suit your needs. All of them charge extra the more contacts you have, but some offer free versions as you build your list. Think long-term, however, if you plan to write more than one book. Chances are your list will grow. Be sure you're prepared for the bigger fees as your list expands.

Currently, companies like Mail Chimp, Constant Contact and Vertical Response are well rated, but there are many others. If you work with a hub author site (I use Writerspace) or use a promotions services company, you might have an option for that group to take over your mailing list. Keep in mind the potential cost savings—not having to pay out of pocket for a separate mail service provider— when considering professional promotional services.

After you've decided on a mailing list service, post sign-up links to your newsletter on your blog, website and in social media venues. Explore the tools available from your mailing list software to see what kinds of tools they offer for publicizing the list. Fans might be able to sign up via text or through a Facebook widget. Take advantage of as many features as you can so that readers never have to look far for a way to connect with you. Mention your newsletter in the end notes of your book so readers know how to find out more about your work. Consider running a promotional giveaway so that the first 200 subscribers are eligible for a prize.

One note of caution about building your subscriber base – don't add readers unless they want to be added. While your newsletter software may allow you to add lists of subscribers at one time, you don't want to add readers unless they've specifically asked to be included. For one thing, you pay for having more subscribers, so it makes better sense to pay for readers who are actively engaged with you and might buy your book. In addition, you want to streamline your mailing list to followers who truly care about your news and will support your releases.

A nice benefit of controlling your own mailing list is the access to analytics about click-through rates and your most popular features. Use these tools to gauge reader interests and tailor content accordingly. As you begin to see more click-throughs on features about pets or kids, offer more pieces of that variety. If your readers are responding to your book reviews or to articles with a humorous tone, pay attention to those cues.

Be wary of sending out too many newsletters or notifications

Leveraging the Mailing List

Once you've got a newsletter in place and are actively building the subscriber list, you can begin reaping the benefits of a dedicated fan base. Now is that time when you'll realize the rewards of including only the fans who have expressed an interest in your work. Try mailing out a newsletter on the day of your next release. Chances are, you'll see a nice bump in sales.

Be wary of sending out too many newsletters or notifications, however. Readers are quick to unsubscribe from a mailing list that clutters their inbox with too many communications. Think carefully before you send material to your readers more than once or twice per month. Consistent, thoughtful contact is better than frequent updates as you think of things to share! Save your news and send readers a well-crafted, interesting update from your writing world.

Book Video

Another option for promoting your release is a book video. There are pricey options available, but if you have a little time and creativity, you can try making your own book video. For some authors, working in a new creative medium can be recharging, whether it's collaging, storyboarding or journaling. Video creation can function the same way.

Think about the kind of story you want to tell in a trailer. Some authors don't summarize the book, choosing instead to simply publicize the release with a video about something else (Gary Shteyngart's videos are notable examples of this approach). Review samples online to find the styles that appeal to you and will work for your book—light and humorous, dark and moody, sweeping epic fantasy? If you're attempting a less traditional book video, utilize the strength of your voice and perspective to create something uniquely engaging but bear in mind the ultimate goals of building your brand and selling books.

Craft a script of no more than two minutes, especially for your first attempt. Give some thought to what copy you'd like narrated versus what you want to appear in print on the screen. You might borrow the tag line from your cover or verbiage from your blurb, but the most traditional format is to set up the basic story conflict. You might end with a leading question or a cliffhanger line that hints at the black moment, but you want something compelling enough to drive readers to buy the book. We listen to story copy differently than we read it, so be sure to read your script aloud to hear how it sounds. Envision the footage with the script so you can start to hear if it will work.

If you have the skills and ambition to shoot your own footage, that's great as it saves a lot of searching through royalty-free images to use in the video. Many authors are limited to stock video and photo footage however. I recommend setting a budget for what you can afford to spend on images and stick to it. If you start spending a lot on the images, you could have simply paid a professional to make the video for you! Sites like iStockphoto are a good place to start searching for images, but don't buy any until you are certain what you need and are committed to your script. If your budget is such that you need the images to be completely free, start with Creative Commons or Flickr. Remember that *not all* the images here are free so you must keep that requirement in mind as you search!

Programs like Windows Movie Maker can create effective videos. You don't need high definition footage. Often, the videos are viewed in small screens on You Tube or through embedded links on your website or social media pages.

If you shoot some of your own footage, be sure to ask for signed "release" forms from the people you use in the video. Generic release forms can be found online and prevent your neighbor from suing you for using her image without authorization. This step is especially important for YA authors who may be using teens in a video shoot. To be safest, you should have the teen's parent sign off on the release form.

Music adds a lot to a book video so don't skip this step. There are some great royalty-free musical pieces available online, they just require some searching. Check into 300 Monks or Soundsnap, making sure whatever you choose is royalty-free so that you only pay to license the music once for the video. Again, if you need the music to be completely free of charge, start with Creative Commons Music and see what you can find.

Lastly, work out your timing. Having assembled all the necessary pieces for your trailer, you'll be in for a long afternoon of editing it all together for the most impact. You can add, shorten or change, but it's worth the extra time to revise the trailer until you're certain it's really strong. If you don't enjoy the experience, there's no need to make a trailer for future books. But if you've discovered a fun and creative way to experience your stories, you'll know this is a good way for you to promote. Upload your video to YouTube and start spreading the word that it's available, or save the book trailer release to coincide with another online event like a cover reveal or a pre-order incentive.

Advance Reviews

Three months prior to release may be enough time to ask a writer friend to blurb your book, depending on the publishing timeline. If you're self-publishing, this gives you plenty of time to add the quote to your artwork, and even small presses usually print final copies close to the release date. Check with your editor to find out when they need a quote to include it on your cover.

Once you're certain the printing schedule allows you enough time, you can think about who to approach to blurb your book. That doesn't mean you should email a copy to the bestselling author of your genre, whom you've never met. It means you can test the waters with writers who have been supportive of your efforts to publish and see if they would be amenable to reading and reviewing your book for you in advance of publication. This is where professional networking pays off. Think about the other writers you've met at conferences or online, authors with whom you've critiqued, or perhaps authors you've featured on your blog.

There is an etiquette for this process. If you are working with a traditional publisher, ask your publicist or editor to help you brainstorm who to approach. They may already have authors in mind and, as an added bonus, they may be prepared to ask another author on your behalf. If not, shape your list based on your editor's feedback and then consider the most tactful approach. If you don't have a close relationship with the author you hope to ask, you can query the author's agent to find out if their client is amenable to the request.

Don't take it personally if the author declines ... Accept their decline graciously and professionally

Be careful when framing your request so that you accurately depict what you're asking for. Don't give an author the impression their quote will go on your front cover if it will be on an inside page. A cover quote has additional prestige and visibility. Ask one person at a time for a cover quote so you don't inadvertently book that spot twice. While that may sound like an enviable position to be in (two cover quotes!) it isn't worth the potential risk to a professional relationship if someone feels slighted in the process. Lastly, don't take it personally if the author declines. Often, authors are simply too overworked to devote the time to offering a quote. Accept their decline graciously and professionally. And for the authors who do provide quotes, be sure to send them a handwritten thank you note. Some even go so far as to send a token gift in thanks, such as chocolates.

Advance reviews are helpful for generating early buzz. Include them on your website, in your promotional literature, and anywhere you tout the book. A mention in your acknowledgements might be a nice way to say thank you as well. Send a copy of your book or bookmark to show the author how their quote looks on the cover or in use on your promo items. Popular authors receive many requests for blurbs and the demand on their time to offer this is considerable. Any "extra" promotion you can offer a supportive author is a nice way to thank them for their time.

Web Presence: Three Months Prior to Launch

Three months prior to your book's release, your web presence should be growing. Are you updating the content regularly? Have you added a blog or an RSS feed from your Tumblr or from a group blog where you contribute regularly? Did you add a sign up box for readers to opt into your mailing list?

If you haven't implemented a system for measuring your web traffic, you should do this as soon as possible. Google Analytics is free, easy, and helps you see which pages on your website are drawing the most visitors, how visitors search for you online and what kinds of features have the most engagement.

Now think about how you can grow your content and target it more specifically to visitors' interests. What trends have you seen in the topics your readers discuss in social media? This helps show you what your followers are interested in. What do you have to say on those topics?

As a historical author, you might share interesting snippets from history whether that means posting a regular historical fashion photo or a bit of drama from the royal court during the period you write. Likewise, consider any expansion of a topic that interests you and your readers.

Discussion Guide

One possibility for increasing the depth of your content could be offering discussion guides for your stories. If you write the kinds of stories that a book club might choose, for example, why not create your own reading guide for fans to download and use in their discussion. There are plenty of tips available online for how to do this or use other discussion guides as samples to walk you through the process. There is a nice article on bookbrowse.com on DIY Discussion Guides that can get you started.

Educational Resources

If you're writing Young Adult books or non-fiction pieces that might be used in the classroom, you will enhance your web presence if you add some educational resources to use in conjunction with your book. For the series I wrote as J.K. Rock, my writing partner, **Karen Rock**, drew on her years as a teacher to align some book activities with the common core standards. She made her resources available on the series' website and we mailed copies to school libraries as well.

Bonus Reads

Readers will visit your site for bonus material related to your stories. Do you have a deleted scene from your book that you can post as a free read? Make it available on your website. Better still, offer a free short story or novella that acts as a companion piece to your latest book. Free bonus content sends traffic your way and engages your readers. If one deleted scene gets a lot of hits, it doesn't hurt to brainstorm extra scenes that could have been in the book and write them from scratch. Release the content on an advertised schedule so readers can anticipate the fun of a new scene. Or create a scene countdown before your book's release with episodes leading up to the prologue.

Extras

Some authors post recipes for foods mentioned in their books or pictures of a research trip that helped them develop the setting.

Whatever "extras" you offer your readers, make sure to keep the content fresh with frequent updates. You can design special digital badges with images of your characters (remember to use your own photography or to properly license your images) that visitors can download and show off on their own sites and in social media. Anything a visitor can print out is great too. Offer special contests on your website or recurring monthly giveaways.

The One-Month Launch Plan

If you're writing hard and fast and need to limit the amount of time you spend promoting your book, here's a quick list of some promo ideas that you can arrange in a hurry. Keep in mind, you can always try to solicit some promo help from a virtual assistant or a family member to tackle some of the items. *USA Today* best-seller and RITA Award winner **Catherine Mann** suggests, "Enlist family members to post for you during deadline crunches. Make sure that person identifies herself/himself in the postings. This offers fans another opportunity to enjoy being a part of your world – an insider's peek."

You will notice many of the suggestions during the One-Month Plan are "event" oriented. This reflects your movement toward the actual release date. Ideally, the relationships you've built through the year will help you as your book becomes available. Promotional efforts this month require more concentrated involvement as you host live and cyber events to generate buzz and increase awareness for your release.

- Blitz event
- Targeted social media events
- Book signings
- Street team efforts
- Special promotions
- Web presence: One month prior to launch

Blitz Event

One of the quickest ways to spread the word about your book is to organize a book blitz event. This is different from a blog tour in that it requires less content creation. Whereas a blog tour features a range of excerpts from your book, author or character interviews, Q & As, and thoughtful blog articles that you generate, a blitz event simply posts your cover, blurb, purchase links and author information on participating blogs during your release week or during the time frame of your choice.

A blitz is less expensive than a blog tour and if you don't have much time to promote, you may appreciate the chance to let a professional handle this portion

Blog tour companies often organize blitz events in their menu of services. Scan your favorite blogs to find out which tour companies they work with and contact them for their rates. A blitz is less expensive than a blog tour and if you don't have much time to promote, you may appreciate the chance to let a professional handle this portion of your efforts. In addition, the tour companies have many more blogger contacts than most authors, so they can reach a wider audience than if you put out a private call for sign-ups on your social media links.

However, if you're strapped for budget and want to try organizing the blitz on your own, be ready to design a nice blitz banner and an online sign-up form. Google Docs has a great program for the sign-up sheets. Post the details about the blitz on your blog or website, then link to the details *and* the sign-up form in your social media announcements. If you have a handful of blogger friends, you can ask them for advice on other bloggers to approach, or you can ask your local writing community for help spreading the word to bloggers who might be interested.

Once you have some bloggers signed up to participate in the blitz, be timely in delivering the information they need to upload a page about your book. This means sending material 3-7 days before the event begins. Be sure you collect all the information in one place for one email so your participants have all the resources they need in one spot. As always, be courteous and professional, thank them for their participation, and show your appreciation by linking back to their blogs.

Targeted Social Media Events

Elsewhere, we have briefly discussed the benefits of developing a social media presence. Now, let's look at some more ways to use those tools as your release date draws near. If you've been engaging in social media regularly in the months leading up to your book's launch, you should be coming more familiar with the added opportunities on each one.

For example, Facebook Pages and Profiles both allow you to create an event, as does a Goodreads Author profile. Use these tools to announce your book release as an event. Add your cover art to the event page and invite people you've connected with online.

You can also create a live event online by scheduling a Facebook party or Twitter party.

Goodreads has an "Event" option for authors that you can use as a base for an online launch celebration. It's easy to search directions on how to set up an event at any of your social media sites. Once you've decided where you'd like to host a party, think of it in terms of a real event. Think about food to serve and decorations to use, all of which can reflect the book's theme, setting, or main character.

Posts with photos or video usually receive twice as much engagement as text posts

Take pictures of the food and décor to make the party come alive. Post pictures intermittently during the party to maintain interest. Posts with photos or video usually receive twice as much engagement as text posts. Make sure the event banner is unique. Schedule posts throughout the party so the forum is never quiet for too long. You can invite other authors to post with you if you have friends who write in your genre. Offer periodic giveaways.

If you opt for a Twitter chat, the event is less structured but the same rules apply. Decide on a chat hashtag and ask guests to use it during the event to keep track of posts. A dashboard like Hootsuite makes events like this much easier to manage as you can set up streams for keywords and the chat hashtag.

Think about different ways to engage your readers according to the distinct features of each network

Multi-pronged Approach

As you plan your social media outreach during the month leading up to your release, think about how you can connect with readers using the unique tools and appeal of the individual social media sites. In other words, don't just run a contest on your blog and post it on all your social media. Of course, you *can* do this. But you'll make better use of your diverse social media presence if you also think about different ways to engage your readers according to the distinct features of each network.

For example, when my YA writing partner, award-winning author **Karen Rock**, and I thought about ways to launch our first Young Adult series as J.K. Rock, we developed a plan that allowed for unique interaction on each of our social media sites. For Goodreads, we created a trivia quiz for our novella, *Camp Kiss*, and offered a prize to a random quiz-participant. On Tumblr, we posted our blog tour giveaway but gave a bonus prize to someone who re-blogged the page. This gave other Tumblr-bloggers incentive to re-blog the piece and helped disseminate the message. For Pinterest, Karen created a themed countdown of camp-related photos and we gave a prize to one random re-Pinner. We made our website the central location for information about all the promotional giveaways.

This multi-pronged approach helped us appeal to social media users in the formats they enjoy most and took advantage of each venue's unique tools. The method generated impressive traffic for authors writing under a virtually unknown pseudonym and helped to build our fan base. The only expense came in the cost of prizes and the postage to ship them to winners.

When it comes to prizes, a picture is worth a thousand words. Don't just announce your giveaway in so many words. Take a photo of the prize and post it online. This increases interest, engagements and contest entries. Plan your budget carefully when you offer prizes internationally as it's very expensive to ship overseas. You can send books to international winners through places like Better World Books or Book Depository where global shipping is free. That's a great cost savings, but it takes away your chance to send the winner a personal note or swag items.

Rafflecopter

Many authors use Rafflecopter to organize their giveaways and ask fans for Likes, Follows and Shares in a variety of social media forums. The Rafflecopter site bills their tool as allowing you to "to customize and embed an entry form on your site that incentivizes your audience to perform tasks in exchange for entries into a sweepstakes." Rafflecopter drawings are easy to set up and you can create an account for free. They generate easy to use tools for your giveaway that help you share them easily. As of this writing, they are popular and well-used, but do be careful of employing tools like this too often as they can come across as making demands of your readers.

Balance Rafflecopter-style giveaways with prize opportunities where the drawings are open to everyone.

Book Signings & Other Author Events

Once the book is available, you have the option of scheduling book signings or other author events that offer you a way to personally connect with readers. If you're writing Young Adult books, that might mean visits to school libraries or to individual classrooms. Some authors coordinate Skype events with teachers as well, giving you a chance to visit with student readers without the expense of traveling.

In addition, there are reader events like ThrillerFest or Comic Con that attract lots of dedicated fans in one place. For a more complete listing of book festivals, check out readerevents.com

CEO of In Focus Brands, **Robert Manasier**, reminds clients that, "If you can be in front of people and share a piece of yourself via book readings, storytelling times at bookstores, schools, libraries, events as a volunteer will give you market feedback and possibly some local press and sales. If being the center of live attention isn't your style, posting/blogging relevant content, contributing your expertise on answer boards may start the awareness building for your book as long as you can lead them back to your product for sale."

This is a critical reminder at this stage. There's no sense scheduling promo opportunities for yourself that will make you uncomfortable. Know your strengths and play to them. If you haven't ever done an author signing, by all means, you should! But if after one you feel like your time could be better applied to your work in progress or through connecting with readers in a social media setting, that's helpful information to use when planning your next book's release.

A good live event benefits from strong visuals in the form of a poster or banner (you can order an inexpensive custom vinyl banner online), some interesting table displays with your bookmarks, small giveaway items, flyers about you and your work, business cards or teaser cards for upcoming releases. Decorate your table with other book covers in clear acrylic frames so they stand upright. See the section on Live Events in the "One Year Plan" for more ideas for support materials to bring to these events.

If you're selling books through a bookstore, you will need to contact the bookseller in advance to arrange the signing. This is easier to do at a smaller, independent bookstore as the chain stores may require you to obtain permission from their regional headquarters. Even independent stores are often particular about which authors sign and when, often opting for group signings that will generate more traffic. However, if a bookseller is enthusiastic about having you sign your latest release, that's wonderful news. They order your books for you and take care of the sales.

If you coordinate a signing event yourself outside of a bookseller, be sure to have a method of accepting credit card payments like Square™ (squareup.com) that takes a payment through your phone. Check out their list of compatible devices to see if this is feasible for you, keeping in mind you lose a small percentage of profit in the form of a credit card fee. Most authors find this a small price to pay for the additional sales and added convenience for their readers.

Book Signing Alternatives

Another option for signing books is to offer readers a virtual book signing. Some authors opt to do this in conjunction with a new release so that when books are ordered through an appointed bookseller, the books will be signed by the author before being shipped to the customer. Many authors who participate in this kind of signing allow readers to request personalized messages, although some limit personalization to a first name. To set one up, visit your local bookseller to see if they would be willing to work with you on this promotion. If you decide to offer this kind of perk to readers, be sure to add a page to your website explaining the rules and outlining the "how-to" so fans understand how the signing works.

A virtual signing is different from digital book signing, which refers to an author autographing an ebook. There are several companies that allow authors to do this, including AuthorGraph, Autography and MyWrite. Participating authors can provide readers with digital signatures and personalized messages on ebooks, giving authors another way to connect with their fans.

Book Signing Checklist

- "Signed by the Author" stickers
- Table cloth
- Table décor
- IPad or Tablet on display if you have a video to share
- Picture frames holding your covers
- Banner
- Change if you're selling your own books and accepting cash payments
- Method of accepting credit card payments if you're selling your own work
- Copy of your most recent newsletter
- Sign-up sheet for mailing list
- Bookmarks
- Promotional literature
- Business cards
- Giveaway items
- Candy
- Pen for signing
- Sharpie or marker that will write on high gloss bookmarks
- Door prize to raffle off at the end of the event
- Tickets or some way to collect entries for door prize

Street Team Efforts

If you don't have a dedicated promo group working with you, don't skip this section. Some of the suggestions for street team efforts can be undertaken by friends and family who are ready to help you spread the word about your new release.

First, build excitement for your release among your core followers by sharing exclusive excerpts from the upcoming book. You can share your cover art with them the night before the official unveiling or share your book video with the group first. Some authors give street team members the opportunity to be beta readers or give them access to advance copies of the book. Choose whatever strategies feel most comfortable for you and the size of your team, but do generate some buzz in the group first.

Then, poll the group for the kinds of tasks they can help you with. Some members may have access to their local libraries and booksellers and would be happy to drop off small stacks of bookmarks at these places. Other members may have big social networks or dedicated book blogs where they will tout your release, interview you, or otherwise leverage their connections to share news from your writing world.

Get to know your group so you can request tasks that will be the most fun and easy for them. You may discover members who enjoy playing with digital graphics that would love to create web icons of your characters or new banners for your website. Ask if there is any interest in fan-generated book videos so that your story has multiple videos online, contributed by team members. You don't know what kinds of talents are there until you ask.

Be sure to reward team members with exclusive content and access to fun perks from your writing world. You are building a supportive community within the group, and in exchange the group can enjoy a front row seat for watching a book come to life. Always hold up your end of this bargain.

Keep in mind promo groups may disband between books. This is fine and normal, and many authors like to organize fresh street teams for various projects or series so that more readers have the chance to experience the fun of working closely with the author. If you do keep some of the core members year after year, remember to reach out to them now and again as you have new stories release, but also give them easy ways to bow out gracefully. Your promo helpers are volunteers who are excited about your work, so thank them often, give them ways to stay enthusiastic about working with you, but always allow for organic growth and attrition within the team.

Special Promotions

Launch party

Another way to draw attention to your book during the release month is to organize a special event. This can be separate from your book signing, or it can be in conjunction with a book signing. Brainstorm interesting places or themes that relate to your book.

For *Camp Boyfriend*, my co-author Karen and I held a "camping out" party in conjunction with the local arts center. Teens could sign up for the event and enjoy a mini camp experience complete with s'mores, an "add your own chapter" ghost story, games and a trail mix mini-bar. We painted faces, gave away friendship bracelets and generally celebrated the idea of summer camp, the setting for the book.

The party was a lot of work during release month, but the rewards—beyond getting to share the story with our target audience, which was a huge bonus—came in the local press value, enthusiasm and support that helped us decide to create a street team, and great photo opportunities that put us in a camp setting... just like in our book.

The buzz generated by a real life event increases awareness of your work

A special event gives you a reason to chat online about something other than your book, while closely relating to your story. We created awareness of the event on a Facebook page and made some local media connections while talking about "Camping Out." The buzz generated by a real life event increases awareness of your work.

In brainstorming a special event, think about the places, occasions and unique aspects of your story. If the heroine visits with her girlfriends at a local tearoom, can you recreate the place at a café near you? If you write romantic suspense, could you sponsor a "self-defense" night at an area martial arts studio and work in conjunction with a local women's group? Author **Catherine Mann** plans an "adopt-a-pet" event to celebrate an upcoming book from her "Second Chance Ranch" series which features an animal shelter. An event like this can be held at a local dog park in support of an area animal shelter– people who bring bags of dog/puppy or cat/kitten food can be entered to win a large grand prize and attendees are invited to bring their pets. Author **Kelly Hashway**, for her "Touch of Death" YA series, held a "Zombie Prom." Be creative and research what authors in your genre have done.

You can also simply hold a launch party at a local restaurant and bar. Provide theme food or drinks, keep things festive, bring books to sell and enjoy yourself! The benefit of holding a book event here as opposed to a book store is the opportunity to generate some media interest with a special theme, the chance to invite more people, and the element of fun implied by a night out.

Promote price drops

If you are self-publishing your book, you know when you're book is going to drop to a promotional price as you've scheduled this yourself. This is one of your most powerful marketing tools and you'll want to really think through how to make the most of it. There are options for paid advertising from companies like Book Bub, where some authors have seen significant results. However, if this is your very first book and budget is still a primary concern, you can promote a price drop via many free newsletters and websites that specialize in announcing free and .99 books to readers.

If you are a traditionally published author, you may not know about upcoming price discounts on your book until they are underway. This, of course, takes away the chance to do advance promotion. It's important to use your social networks to spread the word, however, as soon as you become aware of the discounted book. Tweet shamelessly and ask for RTs. Most of the time, I don't believe in filling your feed with self-promotional messages, but price drops are big news and your dedicated readers want to know about them. Post on Facebook and Twitter and ask for readers to share. This news even warrants a special email message to your newsletter list as it's not promo so much as a way to give back to supportive fans.

Conferences and Readers Festivals

Book launch time is busy and you may be tempted to quit promoting by now. It is healthy for your career to know when to return to the real job of writing. However, if you've got a new series to share with readers or if your travel schedule allows, reader festivals can be a great place to connect with your target audience.

Check for listings by genre to be sure you align yourself with a conference or festival that caters to your readership so you don't end up with an erotica novel in an event geared toward young adults or vice versa. There are festivals geared toward librarians, readers, or teachers, and conferences geared toward readers of small sub-genres, so do some research to find out where's the best place for you and your work. BookExpo America, or BEA can be pricey for new authors, but they now allow indie authors to purchase space and a signing table at the event, so authors have the ability to make their presence felt here. Smaller regional festivals are a good choice for new authors, so do an internet search for reader events in your state.

You may be able to share a table, or at least share travel and hotel expenses with a like-minded author. This helps defray costs and drives more traffic to your table since there is a second author as a draw for readers. If you don't belong to a writers group in your area, search for one on MeetUp.com or through a chapter of organizations like Romance Writers of America or Mystery Writers of America. These groups put you in touch with local writers who may be interested in pooling resources and readerships to save time and money on promotion.

Web Presence: One Month Prior to Launch

One month before your book release, use your website as the hub for all the other events taking place. This is your home base, and should be updated frequently as you announce new contests, book signings, blog appearances, or special features on the site. When you send out messages on social media, you want to drive traffic back to your website so that readers will spend more time with you.

*Make your purchase
links easy to find on your
backlist and be sure to
write compelling copy
about the book you're
releasing next*

Another way to increase website traffic is to offer a new sneak peek to your book each day in the days leading up to the release. Have a contest running on the website and check that all your links are working. Review the section of your website that talks about your work in progress or upcoming releases. When readers discover they like your work, they will visit your site to find out what other books you have out. Make your purchase links easy to find on your backlist and be sure to write compelling copy about the book you're releasing next.

If you haven't embedded your book video in your website, do this now. Upload your digital press kit and be sure the press release talks about your most recent events or signings. Be sure there is a sign up for your newsletter prominently placed and that readers can quickly and easily find out how to contact you.

Check your website analytics and see what pages people are spending the most time with on your website. Brainstorm ways to provide more content that capitalizes on this knowledge. Consider adding your Twitter feed, or a Facebook badge if you haven't already. Can a visitor "like" the page with a Google + account or add a book to their Gooreads "Want to Buy" list directly from your site? Should you find a way for them to leave comments on your website? None of these things are "musts" but they are good tools to think about adding.

In short, prepare your digital home for a big influx of company! Readers want to know more about you and find out what else you are writing. Be prepared to give them a warm welcome.

Words of Wisdom

As you continue to massage your promotional strategies, I will leave you with some wisdom from industry experts. Many, many writers I spoke with talked about the importance of managing your expectations. We've all heard stories about very successful authors who seem to blaze onto the scene with lots of sales right away. But the reason we've all heard about those precious few incidences of quick success is because they are outside the norm. As **Lisa Filipe** of Tasty Book Tours remarked, "You are not going to be Nora Roberts overnight." This is not meant to discourage you, merely to remind you that writing books is a business and the path to success is often slow but consistent growth.

Remember to maintain your writing productivity throughout the month, three months, or year that you spend thinking about your launch plan. Commit your writing goals to paper before you start your promotional efforts, and stick to the plan. Focusing on those goals will help you keep an eye on the most important facet of your work. Keep submitting projects if you'd like to hybrid publish or move into traditional publishing. **Russ Thompson,** Public Relations and Marketing Director of Journalstone Books reminds authors "Don't lose hope. Just because your work wasn't accepted by a publisher doesn't mean that it wasn't good. I read a submission once that was a great story, and it was very well written. The characters were engaging and fully fleshed out. In short, I loved it. Unfortunately, there were other books under consideration that had much higher potential in the markets that we cater to, and the decision was made to not publish this particular book. It is my sincere hope that this author submitted his work elsewhere, and that it was accepted. The lesson here is that no one, from one publisher to agent, should keep you from continuing to push for your work to be published."

While you're writing and submitting, use the between time for researching promotion ideas and testing out a few of your own. If you try some promotional strategies and they don't work for you, choose some different ideas for your next release. Keep your website content fresh and consistent with your brand, but all the other facets of your marketing can be re-evaluated. Try new things and see what works. Build on the areas where you have success. And always, always be mindful that the writing comes first and foremost. Readers truly do find good books. Word of mouth is the most powerful springboard to success and it only happens when you've written something so special that readers can't wait to share it with a friend.

Until then, here are some words of wisdom from authors who have put a great deal of thought and effort into managing successful careers:

Manage your time. It's easy to get drawn into spending more time on social media marketing than you do writing. Be careful not to drain the "word well." Slot times in the day to check in on Facebook. Use times you're sitting in the doctor's office or at a ballgame for Twitter, etc. A great quality book is your best promotional tool so make sure you have the time and energy to devote to core writing. — **Catherine Mann,** *USA Today* bestselling author

Stay educated. The industry is changing quickly and the ways to succeed in traditional and indie publishing are shifting quickly. I'm also a strong believer in never burning bridges. Things cycle and you might want to be in cycle with them. And if you decide you don't need an editor or an agent, what happens when you do?—**Lisa Renee Jones**, *New York Times* bestselling author of the Inside Out series.

Research to find out what is a productive promotion "right now," because what was working six months ago may have already gone away, or it might have gotten better. Authors today have to constantly work to improve their craft, but also put just as much dedication into learning the business in all ways.— **Dianna Love,** *New York Times* bestselling author

I would say my biggest piece of advice is to manage your expectations - and to not expect too much too soon. What do I mean by that? You start a website, build a Facebook page and acquire hundreds of new followers. You're doing everything right. So why aren't your sales where you thought they would be? Or maybe you did everything right and you anticipate everything will take off ... but the fact is - and believe it or not it's taken me over twenty years to learn this - it's a marathon not a sprint. You are in this for the long haul. You need to build book by book. And learn to be happy with where you are at any given time with an eye to the future. – **Carly Phillips**, *New York Times* bestselling author

Make friends. Real friends. Care about your fellow writers. Don't look at them as competition because high water floats all boats. Do stuff for your writer friends not because you'll get something in return, but because self-publishing can be an even lonelier business than traditional publishing because you alone are responsible for every aspect of the production process. Having friends who understand you is worth more than pure gold. And when you really need something, those friends will come through for you. You won't even have to ask. Be a good friend. You'll have no regrets and tons of rewards!—**Julie Leto**, *New York Times* bestselling author

Resources

Banner Makers – Build a Sign or Staples

Business Cards – Vista Print or Staples

Creative Commons – images and music you can use for free

Digital Book Signing tools – AuthorGraph, Autography and MyWrite

DIY Discussion Guides – at the Book Browse website

Educational Resources for Camp Boyfriend – sample of the YA educator materials on the JK Rock website

Frames – display book covers in clear acrylic frames available at Michaels

Google Analytics – tools for measuring your website's traffic and effectiveness

Hootsuite – social network manager that allows you to schedule Tweets and send messages across multiple social media outlets

iStockphoto – royalty-free images

Newsletter services – Mail Chimp, Constant Contact and Vertical Response

Promotional Products – giveaways at Print Globe

Promotional T-shirts – Discount Mugs

Storefront – customize and sell your own designs through your website using Cafe Press

Rafflecopter – allows you to customize your giveaways and embed a widget across multiple sites

Reader Events – lists conferences, festivals, and book signings

Royalty-free music – 300 Monks and Soundsnap

The Square – device for using your phone to accept credit card payments

Windows Movie Maker – tool for creating book videos

Samples and How-Tos

Figure 1 Author Bio Simplified

You've written 200 to 400 page novels, but crafting a few paragraphs about yourself is always intimidating. A bio, or short biography, should relate your background and professional achievements in simple, straightforward prose.

The following skeleton bio is a tried and true "fill-in-the-blank" model to get you going. And you'll find that, once you get some prompting about what to put down on paper, you can write a more eloquent, personalized bio than this one. It is certainly not the *writing* aspect of this task that presents difficulty, but the awkwardness of touting your own accomplishments.

* The text in regular typeface is actual verbiage to use in your release
* The underlined text is information you fill in accordingly

* The italics text includes my notes to you

Biographical Notes
Your Name

Your Name is a career [*If your primary career is not writing, add writing as additional career [an accountant and writer]*] and has been writing *[or more specific branch of fiction]* for however long.

The author of # of books, Your Last Name [start listing your accomplishments. Talk about awards you've won, stellar reviews you've received, how many languages your books are translated into, etc. Don't be modest! Has a book gone into extra printings? Have you sold a series? This is the paragraph to showcase your best and most recent achievements.]

[*If you wish to stress any other area of strength, this is the place to do it.*] *Example:*

Noted speaker and workshop presenter <u>Your Last Name</u> is also a frequent contributor to <u>any publications you write for</u>.

A native of <u>Your Hometown/or Region</u>, <u>Your Name</u> has resided in <u>Your current home city or region of the country</u> for the last <u>However many years</u> with <u>her/his husband and three children, dog, cats, etc</u>. [*Nice to end on a personal note. Could also include a quote from you here or in a stand-alone paragraph above this one about why you write.*]

Figure 2 Press Release Simplified

Fill in the underlined sections of the following all-purpose press release with the pertinent information. Use this "skeleton" as a guide to write media releases announcing the sale of a book, the release of a book, the re-release or reprinting of a book, upcoming book signings, or other newsworthy information about your career. Gear your release to showcase the uniqueness of whatever information you are releasing– this is meant only as a guide to get you started! Stick to one page where possible, using two pages at the most.

* The text in regular typeface is actual verbiage to use in your release

* The underlined text is information you fill in accordingly

* The italics text includes my notes to you

[Start at the top of the page]

For Immediate Release
or
For Release <u>Date</u>

For Further Information Contact:
<u>Your Name</u> <u>Your Phone #</u>
<u>Social Media Links</u>

Local Resident Announces Sale of First Book [or Release of New Book, etc.]

(<u>CITY</u>) - Local author <u>Your Name</u> sold her first book, a <u>Genre</u>, to <u>Publisher</u> <u>when [last week, this month]</u>. The novel, entitled <u>Title</u>, is due in stores <u>Release Date</u>.

A <u># of years or lifelong</u> resident of <u>City</u>, <u>Your Last Name</u> has been writing <u>Type or Genre</u> fiction for the past <u>Number</u> years. <u>Title of Book</u> is one of <u>Number</u> books she has written, <u>Breadth of your style [ranging the gamut from inspirational romance to historical fiction or all kinds of action adventure stories]</u>. As <u>your other profession</u> at / for <u>your company</u> [if this is not applicable for you, try another interesting fact about yourself], <u>Last</u>

name writes "" quote from you– it could be about how you write, when you find time to write, or why you write.

Title of your book is about Back Cover type Blurb on the basic plot of your book 25-50 words. [Think high concept! You don't want to lose the editor in a lengthy description].

"" Quote from you about why you wrote the book or what inspired you. Could be why you think other people might like the book. Here is a perfect sales pitch opportunity for you! What is unique about your book? Keep this paragraph to a sentence or two.

If you have book signings planned, mention them in an optional 5th paragraph. For example: Last Name plans a book tour for Time Frame and will be appearing at Wal-Marts, Major Booksellers, etc. in Cities targeted. The book is available online link.

Figure 3 Promotion Target List

Brainstorm as many possible places to send your publicity kit, advance reading copies, press releases or all of the above. Don't let cost intimidate you at first– not all of your target outlets need to receive the full-blown fancy press kit. For many places, a press release or personal letter will do the job. Keep in mind not all of these venues may be suitable for your book—ie, you might not want your co-workers to know about an erotica novel or you don't feel comfortable sharing a gritty action tale with your local church group. Use only the suggestions that work for you and for the book.

1. Hometown newspaper. One of your best bets will be the local paper from the town you grew up in or where you live today (if they are different, send to both). Weeklies or small circulation dailies with distinct

local coverage can usually be persuaded to do a small feature

2. Regional newspaper. Besides the small paper that covers the little league games and bridge club meetings, there's bound to be a bigger paper nearby that would be interested in your news

3. Book review section of your regional newspaper. You may need to send separate press kits to the book reviewer to pitch a review and the featured editor or business editor to pitch a story

4. High school newspaper

5. College newspaper

6. Church or synagogue news bulletin

7. Corporate bulletin at work or other in-house newsletter at your place of business

8. Corporate bulletin, company newsletter or bulletin board at your spouse's place of business

9. Local radio stations that host interviews or have a book discussion program

10. Local television stations. Some stations host early morning talk shows with a local slant

11. Newspapers, radio and television in any regions with which you have close ties. Did you live and work in Jackson, Mississippi for several years? Pitch your news there too

12. Local writer's group newsletter

13. Booksellers with whom you have cultivated good relationships
14. Local library
15. Romance review sites
16. Bookstores
17. Send postcards to friends. Friends are great at spreading the word!
18. Readers groups
19. Website for your publishing house or line, if applicable
20. Web mistress for your writer's group if they have a website
21. Writing groups that sponsored a contest you won- they love sharing the good news, especially if your sale came as a result of their contest

Acknowledgements:

This project was inspired by my friend, savvy literary agent Melissa Jeglinski, who suggested I compile my notes from a conference and make them available to other writers online. Thank you, MJ, for the great idea! Also, many thanks to my writing pal, Catherine Mann, who has not only read everything I've ever written, but who continually inspires me to be the best writer possible. Your wise advice has never steered me wrong. Much gratitude to Lisa Filipe for coordinating the inaugural Tasty Authors Weekend and making it such a fun event for everyone in attendance. You—and all the fabulous writers and bloggers that I met—reminded me I have a unique perspective to offer other writers. Thanks for making me feel like a superstar for a few days! Special thanks to my agent, Barbara Collins Rosenberg, for the thoughtful attention she gave this project, helping me navigate the non-fiction terrain. Thank you also to author Sarra Cannon for generously sharing her insights about self-publishing in a way that gave me the courage to try it for myself. Finally, thank you to Fred Antico and the Public Communications department at the College of St. Rose in Albany, New York, for providing the base layer of skills I've added to over the years. I never would have guessed all the ways I'd put my education to work, and thank you so much for giving me a skill set that's remained relevant and useful across the decades.

About Joanne:

Joanne Rock is the author of over sixty romances and, under the pseudonym **J.K. Rock**, she has co-authored a Young Adult series with her sister-in-law. Prior to her writing career, Joanne worked as a public relations coordinator in a private firm and as a promotions director for a small television station. Her undergraduate degree in communications focused on public relations and she's turned to this training again and again as an author to maintain a readership in a competitive and rapidly changing publishing environment. A frequent conference speaker and workshop presenter, Joanne's seminars are often praised for her ability to be clear and succinct while presenting information, a skill she hopes she brings to this book. To learn more about her work, please visit her online at **http://joannerock.com** or on Twitter **@JoanneRock6**